Skip the

Party

START A
BUSINESS

A Good Life Guide to
Purposeful Living, Real Love and
Successful Entrepreneurship

ARIANA PIERCE

Skip The Party Start a Business
A Must-Know Guide to a Good Life, Real Love and Successful Entrepreneurship

ISBN: 978-0-9977656-1-8

Author's Autograph Page

This Book Belongs to:

_____

ARIANA PIERCE

DEDICATION

I dedicate this book to my loving grandfather, Alfred Scott, who pushed me to be the entrepreneur I am today. Your words and legacy live on through me. You taught me to carry a camera, pen and business cards, because that's what every successful entrepreneur needs. I will continue to use my life in a way that inspires others to live their best life, because that's what you did for me.

— *Your granddaughter, Ariana Pierce*

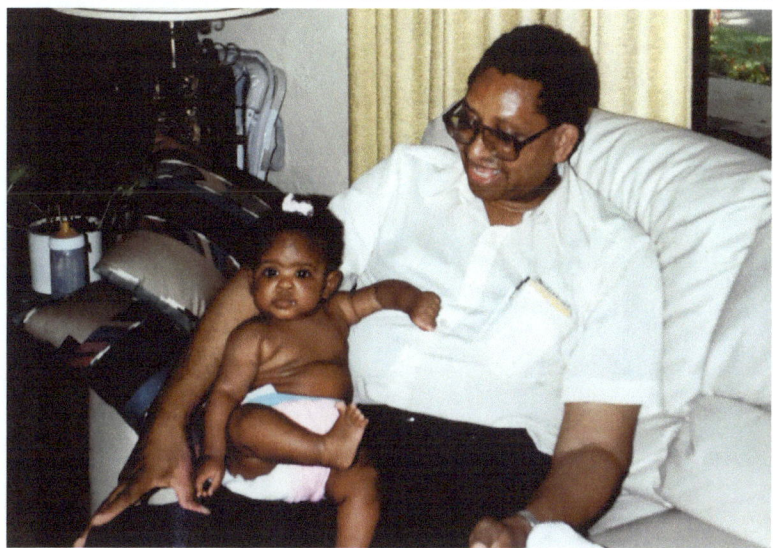

TABLE OF CONTENTS

INTRODUCTION

Every morning, I wake up to pray, meditate and give thanks for all that has happened and will happen in my life. It's so important because it sets the tone for the rest of my day. One day as I was meditating and having quiet time, the idea came to me to share my life story of growing up as an entrepreneur. I thought about the trials, hardships, victories and successes that have happened over the years that people don't really know too much about.

During the years, I heard people say that my life has been a fairytale and that I was just a lucky girl. Let me be totally honest with you: My life has been amazing and I do feel like a lot of what has happened has been a dream, but the reality is, I was very intentional with my life. Nothing just happened for me. I had to work my butt off and be disciplined in areas that are very hard for young people to do nowadays.

My so-called perfect life consisted of getting teased throughout high school. It included battling with my weight and trying to achieve the perfect body. It included trying to find Mr. Right but instead only being with Mr. Right Now. It included getting outside of my comfort zone so that I could be exposed to something new that would change my mindset for the better. That's why I wrote this book; I wanted to share my deepest secrets with you.

As a young person who wants to be successful, there are some choices that you have to make right now in your life that are non-negotiable. Like my dad always says, there are some mistakes you can't afford to make when you want to be a success in life. Now, this isn't to condemn you or say that if you've made a bad choice in life, then you can't live your dreams. What I mean is that right now in your life, no matter your past, you are going to have to stand tall and say with your heart that you will live a life that yields successful results. It means that there are going be times when you have to stand alone from the crowd and choose to go a different direction that isn't so popular.

One thing that I want you to note when you Skip the Party, and Start YOUR Business, is that there may be some teasing, embarrassment and distractions that will try to come your way. After sharing so much of my life growing up in this book, I realized that success really doesn't come easily. And by that I don't even mean that working on your business is hard. I mean the obstacles that are thrown your way when trying to succeed can be the tough part. I remember wanting to be cool and accepted by my peers so badly. Like any other young person, having your peers' approval is the world. Even with all that, I decided to stay on the straight and narrow path to victory and success in business. What made me live this type of life had to do with several factors including having the right mentors, listening to my parents, reading success books and setting my intentions on the right outcomes.

In this book, I'm going to show the steps it took to really become who I am today. There will be personal things shared that may surprise you. I don't want you to be so marveled by the stories that you don't get the real point of me sharing them. They are there to give you inspiration and hope to starting your business and living your best life now. At the end of most of the chapters, there are activities for you to do. Take action on each of them quickly so that you get the best results and outcomes. Don't wait until you are entirely done with the book, or even wait for weeks after to do the homework. It's provided to change your current habits into ones that will get you on course.

So let's get going on this journey to starting or building your successful business!

CHAPTER 1

MY MOTHER'S INFLUENCE

My biggest dream growing up was to be like my mommy. With her strong and bold personality, I could see myself being just like her one day. From her stylish clothes to her entrepreneurial background, I knew that I had a lot to live up to. I remember her and my father taking care of our family store at the local mall. It was a makeup shop called Riana's Cosmetics, inspired by my name, Ariana. The products sold consisted of custom foundation, blushes, and all things makeup. The store was a hit, and my favorite place to be on a Saturday morning was right there with my mom. I would watch her consistently make runs to the store, giving the customers a great experience. There were beauty classes where she would teach ladies how to apply their makeup, wear the right clothing that fit their bodies properly, and even etiquette tips that would cause them to achieve more in life. Later she became a life coach, but this was the first time I witnessed her coaching ladies to not only look their best, but to feel and be their best.

Her biggest thing over the years is that image is everything. She would say it at home and at the office. Whether she was talking to me or to a girlfriend, she stressed the importance of looking good and taking care of yourself every single day. I believe this message sparked my love for fashion and beauty. Over the years I discovered that your image educates others on how to treat you. Whether that's positive or negative, it's the reality we live in today. People treat you as well as you treat yourself. This concept would later spark the idea to create Superstar Nail Lacquer, our nail lacquer brand, which would allow ladies everywhere to feel good and beautiful.

My mom has always pushed me to be my best and be creative. When I was a little girl, I remember putting on a play for the adults at my church. I was about 10 years old, and my mom told me that if I wanted to put on a play, I needed to come up with a marketing plan and sell tickets. Well of course, my marketing plan was "door to door" sales, also known as going up to people after church and asking them if they wanted to buy a $5 ticket to our show. The plan worked, and we were off to selling our first stage production. This practice of creating a play, selling tickets and making money helped me develop a love for true entrepreneurship. I would like to believe that this was her plan to get me rolling on the path to successful entrepreneurship.

Work Hard, Play Harder

My mother has always believed in the idea of raising your children toward the way they are bent, or their level of creativity. I was always the one who loved entertainment, fashion and travel. One thing I love about how my brother and I were raised is that our parents would buy us books, gifts and toys that had to do with our purpose and love at the time. When I was able to pick up a book and read, my mom discovered that I loved putting on productions, selling things and doing lemonade stands. Because of that, she began to buy me children's books on selling and buying, such as how to set up a killer lemonade stand, and biographies from kids who had achieved a lot at a young age.

Like most kids, I wanted to do things other than read a book, like play with friends and watch my favorite TV show. My parents understood that, so they created a reward system that caused us to want to read a lot more. For every 10 books we read, we would be rewarded with an allowance to get a toy or do whatever we wanted with it. It was an awesome deal as a kid, and I couldn't wait to get to American Girl to buy my next doll to add to my collection.

What I didn't realize at the time was the lesson this reward system was teaching me. For every 10 books, I would get an allowance. This made reading more enjoyable knowing that on the other side of finishing, I would be able to get a toy or something that I really wanted. It also taught me that things don't come free. You have to put in something to get back something. I think that's what is missing a lot from our generation today. We want things handed to us without putting in much work and that's just not how things operate. If you want to be successful and build a great name for yourself, you are going to have to contribute something great to this world. It was a valuable lesson that both my parents taught me, which I still practice to this day. That's why I wrote this book—I wanted to give you not only my story, but also the keys for successful living in business. When you work hard, you can truly play hard.

Lessons from Grandpa Scott

One of my other big influences growing up happened to be my grandfather, Alfred Scott. He was from a small town in Michigan and had lots of ambition. I remember him telling me stories about how he had to walk miles to school to get an education. His biggest advice to me was to read, read, read. As a matter of fact, every time a grandkid would ask him a question about anything, his first response was that there was a book on that subject. He would miraculously show up the next day with a book concerning the question we had. It was phenomenal. This taught me the importance of reading daily and how answers to life's biggest questions could be found in books.

My grandfather would always tell me that a real entrepreneur always has a pen and camera on him. (Now this was way before the cell phone was being used.) He would literally buy me a pack of pens and a Kodak camera to put into my bag while we were on the go. So here I am, 6 years old, taking pictures of everything I could see: The ducks in the water, the fountain, beautiful buildings, and pictures with family and friends became something I captured every single day. What I didn't know was that this was right in line with my future and purpose.

Fast-forward to the present, and I make a great living off of my photos and social media. I'm forever grateful for the principles he instilled in me, because they made me into the person I am today. I love you, Grandpa!

Daddy's Lessons

I'm a daddy's girl at heart. Growing up, I always felt a close bond with my father. He has been there for me since the age of one, and has always treated me like his own. There was never a stepdad type of vibe, but only a daddy vibe. He would tell me how beautiful, special and smart I was every single day. I believe this helped me to build my self-esteem and be a strong leader today. As I became a teenager, he would remind me how important it was to carry myself in a mature and ladylike manner.

There was one conversation that changed my life forever and caused me to stay on the straight and narrow. My father sat me down in our kitchen and said, "I want you to remember one thing. You may decide that you want to be president one day. Never do anything that will tarnish your character or forfeit your chances of running for that office."

In the moment, I looked at him with shock. Did he really believe I was going to be the next president of the United States? Me, Ariana Pierce, touch the world in that big of a way? Because I loved my dad so much, I believed and held on to every word that he said to me from that day forward.

It sticks with me every single day that I wake to make decisions in my life. I always think back to that conversation, and though I may not be the President of The United States (yet), my role as president and leader of my own business is just as important. Having a clean and good reputation has taken me far and I couldn't thank my father enough for encouraging me.

Now, don't feel bad if you have done some wild things in your past. None of us are perfect, but I want to encourage you to hold on to these words from here on out. Think about your decisions and how they can affect your future. You can't change the past, but you sure can change the outcome of your future by making the right decision today!

Though all these people had a great influence in my life, there are still choices that I had to make every single day. I could either follow the path to greatness or follow the path to an average, mediocre life.

To The Parents

The influence of a parent plays a large role in a child's life and perspective. Now this doesn't mean that you can't have different views from your parents, but it does mean that when done the right way, a parent's influence can create habits that lead to success in life. I know this to be true in my own life. I can vividly remember a moment I had with my mother at the kitchen table. We were sitting in our very first home and I was about 7 years old. She created this vision planner where you could paste down photos and words concerning what you wanted your life to be like. This was way before the idea of visualization and manifestation became popular and mainstream.

As we sat in the kitchen pasting down photos of what we wanted in our future, my mom excitedly tore out a picture of Dolce & Gabbana boots from the pages of her fashion magazine and began to cut them out. I looked over and asked her about the boots. She said that they were a designer shoe and the price on them was a whopping $900. Now when I was 7 years old, that was a big number to me, and could be a very big number to a lot of people. I responded with a big, "WHOA." She told me that these would be the kind of shoes she would wear one day and would soon be able to pay for them easily. Fast forward five years later, and my mom was in the Dolce & Gabbana store buying her first $900 shoes with ease. Everything she had written down was manifesting in her life. Business had prospered over the years, and she was able to wear and buy the items she desired. This was a big deal for me being that I had seen my mom write and visualize these things and they had now become her reality.

Now, you may think this is not a big deal, but this lesson helped me to learn the art of dedication and consistency. Though my mom had pasted down these things in her dream planner, she didn't just leave them to happenstance—she took the proper action. She worked her business every single day. When things got tight, she didn't give up or complain; she created a new marketing or business plan until she found what worked. She had a fighter's attitude that no matter what, she was going to be successful at all she put her hands to.

As I started my own business, I put into play the same practices from my mom, like the habit of visualization, affirmation and manifestation, which helped me to jumpstart my business. This planted a seed in me to follow in her footsteps, so I believe this is what helped me to stay focused on my track to success.

The Art of Visualization

Visualization is so important to your success in life because it's a way to keep your focus on the prize. It's a proven fact that what you think about and focus on the most, you begin to attract and manifest in your life, whether you like it or not. Visualization can be easy once you know what to do and how to do it. When I first started to practice the art of visualization, it was hard to keep my mind from wandering off. I would begin focusing on my desired outcome, then my mind would drift off to random thoughts about my day. I had to get a hold on this by changing the way I did this practice. Instead of trying to meditate for an entire hour, I took 15 minutes a day to just think about what's next in my business. What new deals do I want to do? Where do I want to travel for business? What type of sale should I put out there that is creative and new for my audience? Even though my visualization time was shorter, I was getting more done and having better results because I was intentional with what I really wanted in business.

Thoughts really do become things. If you constantly think negative, you will get negative results. If you decide to think positive about your future and business outcomes, that's exactly what you will get too. Don't focus so much on being perfect with your visualization and affirmations, because that's when frustration and disappointment will happen. Instead, enjoy the process and always think of what the best outcome will be, and I promise that you will begin to live the life of your dreams!

From a child's perspective, I want to charge the parents to be an example to their children, especially those who are entrepreneurs. Your children follow more of what you do than what you say. Your actions right now are helping to shape their outcome. This means that you have to continuously push and move forward, no matter what the circumstance or situation in business. Show your kids that the entrepreneur's lifestyle can be fun, exciting and profitable if you keep striving for greatness.

Activity/Assignment: Five-Year Vision Board

In this chapter, I talked about how visualization, affirmation and manifestation played a major part in helping me to stay focused and on track for success. So for this assignment, I want you to create a vision board for where you see yourself in the next five years. Paste down words and pictures that represent what you want to happen in your life and business. It can be millions of dollars, inventions, positive words and even people you'd like to have in your network. Once you are done, I want you to say the affirmation on the next page every morning. If you focus, believe and continuously affirm this, then you will be on your way to huge success. Now, you may look at this affirmation and think that it's the farthest thing from the truth. That's OK. How you change your current truth is by on-purpose focusing on a new and better one. So no matter what your circumstance looks like, believe that there is bigger and better for your life from this day on.

I, _____, am a focused, driven and dedicated entrepreneur. I have amazing business ideas and my marketing mind is like none other. My business is flourishing and I'm a huge success. I'm thankful for all the opportunities that have come my way that have caused me to be a success. I stay on track and it's easy for me to make the right decisions because I want a successful future. Life is great, my network is great, and my family is great. I'm prospering now! I ask for this or something better to be present in my life for the best.

CHAPTER 2

GROWING UP

B eing born in Grand Rapids and then later growing up in East Lansing, Michigan, was an adventure. This meant going to a Christian school in what seemed like the "country" part of town. I was a black girl in a major- ity Caucasian school, which was absolutely no problem for me. As children we did not see color; we saw each other as friends and playmates. Things were great and I loved being around my peers. As time went on, I decided that I wanted a change of scenery—really, I just wanted to be with my cousin in a new school—so I begged my mom to put me in a public school closer to our home. This was the worst ex- perience of my life! I didn't get along well the students and the teacher seemed to get on me for my beliefs. How much harm could a second grader be? Anyone who knows me knows that I wasn't a troubled or bad kid, but the teacher found ways to scold me. Things weren't very peaceful, so my parents thought it would be best to finish out the year at this school and head back to the private school I came from. After going back, I found myself really enjoying the private school a lot more and making awesome friendships that would last a lifetime.

As time went on, my main objective in school was to get straight As. For the most part, I had all As for every single report card that came home. I was an honor student and I was elated every time I could put a smile on my parents' faces. In my mind, I felt like every kid was striving to do their best and stay out of trouble. What I didn't know was this type of attitude would cause me to be looked down upon and teased.

The Lunch Room

It was the summer after eighth grade and I was getting ready for school. I had a whole week's worth of clothes laid out because I was a big girl now. I went to school and it was awesome to be "grown." I loved my teachers and I could finally be in with the cool high schoolers right? Well one day I was talking in the café with a group of older students and before you know it things began to get a bit heated. We were laughing and joking at first, when all of a sudden, one of the older guys called me out from across the room and said I was fat. First of all, I didn't make any remarks toward him, so I was very confused as to why he would just call me out like that. I guess it was a joke that he thought would make him look cool in front of everyone. Though I pretended to laugh it off, those words hit me like a ton of bricks coming at me. During that time, I was going through a transitional phase where I was a bit chunky. What young person doesn't go through pimples, glasses or weight gain? This literally crushed my spirit and I felt terrible about myself. If a guy like that told me I was fat in front of my friends, what else were people thinking about me?

The School Bus

One day, the sports crew was coming back from an exciting game. We had won and things were great. I found my circle of friends who treated me nicely, loved and adored me. As we were pulling in to the school from a long ride home, one of the seniors on the bus was asking people to do inappropriate things. Being a person who cared about my character, even at a young age, I refused to disobey the instructions set out for this trip. Suddenly, a tall "cool guy" stood up on the bus and said, "Oh, so you think you're better than all of us. You're just a teacher's pet, you little goody two-shoes." Now, as a young girl trying to be accepted by her peers, this was so embarrassing and hurtful. I had never done anything wrong to this guy, yet he wanted to humiliate me in front of all my friends. It's bad enough when an older guy humiliates a younger boy, but it's a whole new level of hurt when an older guy teases and tries to hurt a younger girl. I held in my tears because I was a big girl—I wasn't supposed to cry! I took it in and as soon as I got home, I cried, knowing that these words were affecting my spirit. To add to the story, this was one of the faculty members' sons. He knew that he could get away with anything because his parents were running the school. Wow, what a day.

After crying at home to myself about the teasing and bullying, the words of my father came to me: *Never compromise your character for others. No matter the teasing, no matter the struggle, you do what's right.* And that's exactly what I did. Even though I went to a great school, there were still students who didn't want to do what was right. I remember my first encounter of having a friend get pregnant in school. She was so young and had her whole life ahead of her, until she found out she was going to be having a baby. Now, this doesn't mean that you can't do great things if you have a baby young; I'm just sharing how her experience at such a young age shaped her mentality.

As I grew more mature and started to get to an age of independence, I noticed that my peers wanted to sneak out and party more and more. They would lie to their parents about where they would be. They would have secret relationships that their parents did not approve of, because it brought more trouble to their lives. As I saw these things unfold before me, I realized that I didn't want to have any part of this. How would their lives turn out as a result of doing these things? At the time I didn't know, but I trusted that if I did what was right, I would be a success. I accepted the role of being the good girl who listened, got good grades and pushed really hard to please my teachers and my parents. It wasn't anything my mom or dad could force me to do. It was a decision I made because I wanted something different for my future than what my peers did. What I did know was that bad decisions equaled bad results and good decisions equaled good results, so I chose to go the right way.

Graduating

As my senior year started, I felt excited yet nervous for the next chapter in my life. I was really becoming an adult who would soon be full of responsibilities. During this time, I had started a business and blog called The Billionheir Girls Club. It was a place for girls all around the country to get tips on how to have proper etiquette, how to talk with their parents, how to be respectful to authority and how to always look your best. It included a line that consisted of fashion tees, accessories and books. This was something I put my heart into because I was sharing with other girls the things that helped to keep me on track as a young individual.

It was my first independent business, even though I had been dabbling with entrepreneurship since the age of about 13 years old. The older I got, I began to search for more meaning in my business and life calling. Though The Billionheir Girls Club did me well, at the age of 18, I decided I wanted to create something that fit me at the time. I wanted something bigger in business that I could use to help women around the globe feel good. After months of brainstorming, praying and reading books on business, my mom and I started talking about what it would be like to be in the fashion industry. We had already done makeup, T-shirts and accessories. Those things were great, but it was somewhat of a saturated market unless you were a large corporate brand or had a big name already. We desired to start something unique and different that was still related to the fashion and beauty industry, because it was what we knew best.

As we were in the brainstorming process of creating a new business, my mom came to me one day and told me she had a dream. It's common for her to have dreams, so I was open to hearing it. She said, "You know how we have been brainstorming and trying to figure out how to fit into the fashion industry?" I said, "Of course!" She then began to say, "Well, I had a dream about us starting a nail lacquer line and it should be called Superstar Nail Lacquer." After much researching and scouting manufacturers, Superstar

Nail Lacquer was birthed and launched at one of our annual Women's Success Conferences.

When we announced the new polish line, I felt like a nervous wreck. I began to get butterflies in my stomach and wondered if all the hard work we had put into this project even mattered. The time came for the reveal, and then came the immediate response. Thousands of ladies began to flood our product table to purchase the nail lacquer. It was a smashing success and my heart leaped for joy. I continued pushing the line with my mom until just a few months later, she became so busy that she couldn't do it anymore. I took full ownership of it and I was now running a mature, growing business all on my own.

Activity/Assignment: Are you gearing up for college or the next phase in your life? If so, this is the time to start planning your future. Where do you see yourself in the next five years? What business can you see yourself starting or continuing to work on if you already have one? Whenever you are planning your life, it's good to make a list of "right now" goals: Things that you can see and want to achieve now. List them below in the area provided. Go ahead, I give you permission to dream BIG!

1. _____

2. _____

3. _____

4. _____

5. _____

6. _____

7. _____

8. _____

9. _____

10. _____

Notes: _____

_____

_____

_____

_____

_____

CHAPTER 3

THE DISCIPLINE

During my high school years, I had to develop a discipline about myself in order to really "skip the party," or stay away from trouble. I had a desire to do really well in school with my grades, my parents and with my teachers. It was a goal of mine to be the best in whatever I put my hands to. To do this, I had to make a serious decision to ward off what others thought about me and my choice to do what was right, which was also known as being the goody two-shoe. That one decision to do what was right changed my entire life for the better and I'm going to share with you exactly what I did.

As young people, we can struggle with trying to be accepted with the masses. I believe that peer pressure is one of the toughest issues facing us and we have a choice between whether we will fall for what others want for our lives, or do what it takes in order to be successful. I remember being in school and wanting to be friends with the most popular people. I was never one to do anything bad because of peer pressure, but I did find myself wanting to hang out with and be close to the top people. I thought that would make me more likeable and popular. This mindset started to get me off course from focusing on my business and making an impact on others, to help them build their confidence and self-esteem. Many times as young people, we focus so much on trying to be liked, that we miss windows to be great. High school and college are times when people's opinions really matter to us. The bad thing about that is it can cause us to get off track and lose sight of our destiny.

Being popular and well-known is OK, as long as you know who you are. Never lose sight of your greatness in order to be accepted by someone else. When I finally realized that life would pass me by if I didn't put effort and focus toward my business, I began to put the desire of trying to be accepted behind me. Doing that included building a successful company while others wanted to party. It meant doing my homework on time so I could graduate with honors. It meant me using my weekends to travel to business conferences so I could learn how to grow my business in my late teens and early 20s. Once this happened, friends automatically came because they wanted to know how they too could be successful. Now that I have long since graduated, I find that the same people whose affection I was trying to win now ask me about being successful in the real world. That's the thing: When thinking about life after school and after all the minimal things fade, what will your life be like? I want to encourage you right now to look past the so-called popularity, look past the fear of acceptance, and embrace a rewarding attitude that will cause you to live your dreams now and not later.

Make it your goal that you will be at a place in your younger years that makes people twice your age marvel. There isn't a day that goes by that I don't hear those older than me say how impressed they are with the decision I made to start a business and stay focused on my path. I'm not saying this to brag, but I do want you to know that this can be you. You can be the one to impress the world with your gifts and talents. Remember, it's better to skip the party, and go for starting a business.

Finding Better Friends

It's so true—you become like the people you hang around the most. Your circle of influence determines your daily actions and decisions. I knew that if I wanted to stay on the right path, I had to get friends who also wanted to do good. This is so important for young people to practice and do. Finding people who have similar goals and aspirations as you can mean an amazing outcome in your future.

If you are a parent reading this book, encourage your children to hang around like-minded, spirited kids. If you know your child is mild and very soft-spoken, try to surround your child with other kids who have a similar or compatible personality. This helped me so much growing up when choosing my friends. I remember when I was a young girl and even in high school, my mom would warn me of certain friends. She would say that even though I wasn't a bad kid, if I were to hang around people who were mischievous, I could get in trouble just for the association. Don't be afraid to direct your children and their relationships. They may put up a fight, but you have to push back and stand your ground as the authority in their life. Trust me, they will thank you later in life for your wisdom and guidance.

This actually happened to one of my good friends. He was a great kid who was focused on getting his life on track and going to college. Over time, he started to get careless with his friendships and didn't put much effort into having quality relationships. One night, he was in the car with a few buddies, and thought it was just a regular ride. That night the boys decided to steal some things and guess what happened? They got caught by the police, and all went to jail. Though my friend didn't plan on stealing that night, he was accused of doing so and got a bad reputation just for being associated with the wrong people. This could have totally been avoided by a decision to just hang around success-minded people. The moral of this story is you truly become like the people you hang around.

Who's Influencing You?

Getting around influencers that had my answers and didn't create problems helped to steer me in the right direction. Let's face it: As a young person, if you want to be successful at a young age, you have to ask yourself who is influencing you. The right people will tell you when you are wrong, help you in down times, and steer you in the right direction. Over the years, I created a checklist to determine if the people who had the most influence in my life were really good for me. It has helped me to find good and solid friends who care and are positive. I believe that everyone should have this checklist, so it's provided below to help you identify who has your best interest at heart.

Activity/Assignment:

Friendship Checklist

Take some time to check out your friends by using this checklist. It's important to be honest so you can be sure to have the best outcome.

- ✓ **Are the people around you encouraging you to listen to the authority in your life?**

- ✓ **Do they help you go after your goals and dreams?** *Or do they tell you life doesn't take all of that?*

- ✓ **Do they work hard to complete tasks?** *Or do they always find a way out of responsibility?*

If you answered no to any of the bold questions, then it's time to sit back and evaluate your influencers and friendships. You can either be the bigger influencer and point them in the right direction, or if they are still encouraging you to go the opposite way of what it takes to be successful, then you need to walk away. Walking away doesn't mean you have to be rude to them, it just means you let go of the relationship and grab on to new ones that will help encourage you to flourish.

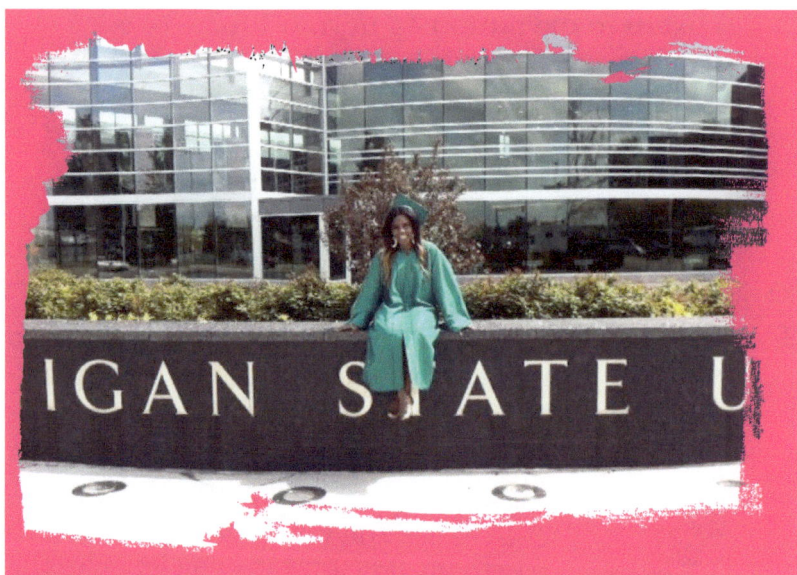

CHAPTER 4

THE POWER OF A MENTOR

With a mentor, magical things can happen in your life. Dreams really do come true when you have someone leading, guiding and influencing you in the right direction. Now, I'm not talking about a friend here. A friend is someone who is more of a companion. By mentor, I mean someone who can speak into your life during the good and bad times. It's important to have a person who can see light years ahead in your business and even in your personal life.

I know this all to be true. When I was in college, I got mentors who understood the college life, but that were responsible and wise. I didn't just confide in "yes" people who were afraid to tell me the truth. They were people who could bring correction to areas of my life that were lacking in discipline. I would go to them for advice on getting good grades in school, since college was so new for me.

I remember my very first semester at Michigan State University. Being that I was a very good student in high school, I figured that the same study habits applied to my college experience and schooling. I received great news that I was able to test out of a few math classes (woohoo!) and move on to calculus. This was great, because I had taken calculus in high school so I was for sure going to pass this with ease. Well, I went through my first semester and it was a bit harder than I thought. For one, the teacher was not American, so their accent was very hard to understand. Why did they have him teaching a calculus class? I don't know, but it was all a mess. I figured I could study like usual and come out with good grades, but that didn't happen. I barely passed that class and my grades were much lower than what I was used to.

At that moment, I went to my mentor and she began to tell me how my approach to this new way of learning and school was wrong. She taught me exactly how I should be studying for my exams and how important office hours with the TA really are. I left myself open to her advice and input because she was an expert in this field. Having an open ear to your mentor's wisdom is important to your success. Every amazing entrepreneur has a business coach, AKA a mentor, so the earlier you catch on to this idea, the quicker you'll see success in your business and life.

One thing that really helped me to succeed at such a young age is sharing my thoughts when something was bothering me. Your mentor should be your sounding board to bounce off your thoughts and ideas. I never ever kept it to myself, and I made sure to have open conversations with my mentors and also my parents. You know a parent can be a type of mentor, too. Appreciating my parents and listening to their wisdom has led me in the right direction every time. This is something that this generation has to get back to doing: showing respect to parents and authority. It can literally save your life.

Activity/Assignment: List Your Mentors

I want you to write a list of people who are or can be positive mentors in your life. They can be people you know or successful people far off who have books and materials you can invest in so you can glean from them.

Having a business coach is so important to your success. No matter how smart or creative you are, you need someone who will lead you in the right direction and correct you when you get off track. Plus, a mentor will help you to become successful much faster when you listen to them. Because they have already been through the things you are dealing with, they can show you how to avoid many of the mistakes that come with being young or new to business.

Create your list below:

My Mentor: Action steps I will take to be a great mentee

1. _____   _____

2. _____   _____

3. _____   _____

4. _____   _____

5. _____   _____

During my junior year of college I was flown in to The Bahamas to speak at a conference. In this photo I was greeted by powerful political figures.

CHAPTER 5

BALANCING SCHOOL AND BUSINESS

S tarting the business is the easy part—staying consistent and actually doing the work is the hard part, especially for someone still in school. As I mentioned in Chapter 2, in high school I had The Billionheir Girls Club, and then when I was graduating and heading to college, I was inspired to create Superstar Nail Lacquer, so I know all too well about having to balance school and a business. What's so funny is that the number one question I receive when doing interviews with media outlets is how I balanced the two and did well in both areas. Usually there is one part of your life that lacks when you are trying to focus on starting a business. My desire was to find a way to be successful at both, so I made sure of some things regarding my schoolwork. I ended up graduating with a very high GPA, and did two study abroad programs, all while growing my business into an internationally known brand. Do you know how this was possible, though? It happened because I had a disciplined and systematic way to get my work done.

Planning for Profits

Being disciplined comes down to planning out your life for a successful business. Like my mom always says, "Nothing just happens until you make plans for it." The number one way I was able to stay balanced with my life while managing a business and trying to finish schoolwork was the daily assignments I would give myself. I made sure to do my homework early during the week and I left the weekends open for business and traveling.

During high school was really where I began to develop these habits and as I matured, things changed, but there were some basic things that helped me to be successful at a young age.

It was a system and routine that I began to develop and it really caused me to be more organized. Organization done the right way can keep your life on course and cause major things to begin to happen for you and your business.

I remember coming home from school and taking a nap. Now, you may be thinking a nap sounds counterproductive for a person who wants to be in business and be successful at it. You're right—it can be. There is a lot of talk about working hard and barely sleeping in order to achieve your goals, and that in order to truly make it, you can't love sleep. This is true to an extent. When you are striving for success and making major moves, there will be times when you have to stay up all night to get a project done. Nights like these are very common when my mom and I are preparing for our International Women's Success Conference. Though we have to get up and speak for three days, we still find ourselves staying up to the wee hours of the night making sure that the binders are set for guests, that the décor is in place and that all our media for the conference is spectacular. In those instances, yes, sleeping is for the birds and your work must come first if you want to put on a successful event.

Now, when it comes to being a young person who is still developing physically and mentally, you need rest. If I felt tired from a long day at school and sports practice, I'd come home and get at least 30 minutes of sleep to refresh myself from a long day. After that, I'd set my clock to do my homework and get it done within an hour—two hours depending on the assignments we were given. After that was finished, I'd watch one of my favorite shows and then call a friend to chat about our day at school. At first, I wanted to stay up late like the other kids and socialize all evening, but getting up in the morning wasn't so easy for me. I had to set this new habit of being disciplined with my schedule because I had finally found what made my day more productive. This helped me to stay disciplined throughout the week and keep Saturday and Sunday open for doing my business. Did I ever want my weekends free? Of course! I was still a teen, but I also knew that I wanted to be very successful, so I did what it took to fulfill my dreams through business.

Schedule in Fun

A part of having a balanced life is making sure to fit in fun and exciting moments. That's what true success is all about: creating memories that will last a lifetime. When I was in college, I would make Thursdays my outing days. If there was a game, I'd go watch it. I'd use that day to hang out with friends and really enjoy life, because come Monday, it was back to schoolwork. I learned that you need a day for yourself. It's what helps you to stay creative and causes you to be stress-free.

I'm still grasping this concept today. Do you ever feel guilty about having fun? It's like all the work you haven't completed is waiting and screaming your name for immediate action. While I was writing this book, I felt the need to work on it every minute of the day. But I had to remind myself that taking time to step away and rejuvenate is best for me to stay creative and on the cutting edge to deliver quality content to all who will read this. It's amazing how easy it was for me to finish this book because I had inspiration to pull from.

Take time to plan out "me" time this week! Plan time away from the computer, away from your next homework assignment, and go somewhere that boosts your creativity and hustle. Go see a good movie or enjoy a nice restaurant with friends. This is a secret that successful people use to keep themselves motivated and ready for big wins in life.

Activity/Assignment: Create a Fun Fund

Like you just read, scheduling in "me" time is important to your sanity and creativity in your business. Now, taking time to enjoy life will require money. You'll need money to pay for a movie ticket, a basketball game or a date night at a fancy restaurant. I want you to create a Fun Fund account where you put away money each week that is strictly for you to treat yourself after a productive week. I usually put away about 5 percent of my income every week, but you can do more than that if you choose. Use this extra savings to reward yourself and experience the good life.

CHAPTER 6

JOURNALING: THE KEY TO SUCCESS

My mother has always said, "What's written is real." I remember having my first diary at the age of 9 or 10 years old. My parents would encourage me to write about my days, dreams I had and toys I really wanted. During that time, I learned the art of journalizing and how it is a key to dream manifestation in my personal life and business.

Once I started my business, I began to use my journal to come up with sales strategies, marketing campaigns and creative ideas. I believe that my brand and business is where it is today because I decided to pen my thoughts to paper. Whenever I get the chance to speak to young, aspiring entrepreneurs, the first thing I tell them to do is get a journal and vision board that allows them to see their desired future. On my vision board, I had pictures of people I wanted to meet, places I wanted my business to take me to, and the amount of money I wanted to make per year. I then coupled this with my journal to expound on the images and desires that were pasted down on my board. It was as if I was writing the chapters to my life's book, and it equaled success. Being specific with my goals was very important to making them a reality. This was something that I learned over the years to see faster and better outcomes.

It's amazing how you can pen something in your journal and over time, see it play out exactly how you wrote it or even better than you wrote it. For example, I was at a place in my life where I wanted to really start getting paid to travel the world. Being a travel blogger was something that fit my overall brand, being that I have a travel line that is doing very well. Instead of trying to contact every person about paying me to travel, I sat down with a cup of green tea and wrote in my journal about why and how I wanted to get paid to travel the world. In depth, I transcribed the places I would visit and how I would share the hot spots in each country on my travel blog. About three months later, a company sent me an email saying that they wanted to pay me to travel and do a review on their products and services. The destination was a place I had never gone before, so excitement filled my heart. I was finally seeing my goals become my reality and my journal was now becoming a place of memories instead of just dreams.

Why It's So Important

Using a journal helps you to crystallize your thoughts and flesh out your ideas. Have you ever tried to keep an idea in your head, and then suddenly forget all the details to it? Yeah, that's happened to me too. Writing things out helps you to develop strategies and concepts that can help your business flourish.

Activity/Assignment:

Grab yourself a journal and begin to write your dreams and aspirations for this season in your life. Use it as a place to daydream about where you want your business to be in the next five years. Writing matters and can add clarity and insight to your project.

CHAPTER 7

READ TO SUCCEED

Reading really is fundamental to your success, no matter what industry you are dreaming or striving to be in. It's that secret that doesn't seem to matter, but actually matters the most. Did you know that successful people read at least one page a day from a book? Why? Because it keeps the mind sharp and it causes you to stay relevant with what's happening in business today. That's what being a millennial entrepreneur is all about, right? Staying relevant and hip to the trending topics at hand.

Reading was something that my parents instilled in me at a very young. When I was younger, I loved to read books on my favorite characters and historical people. Once I became a junior in high school, my reading habits began to go south. It seemed like more and more work was being thrown on my plate that included homework, sports, testing and of course, my business. A book was just an extra assignment that was going to be added to my schedule that I did not want to do. Soon came college and the workload picked up even more. My business was doing great and so I felt that reading success books wasn't necessary. I was reading books for school and I would do that consistently, but books that would really help my business flourish got pushed to the back, and that was not good at all.

What I didn't know was that soon, I would need answers to big questions in my business and life. I could hear my mom's voice telling me that if I would just take some time to read motivational and business books, then I would be growing and expanding my mind to think and actually go bigger in my business. Pondering on this idea, I was reminded of how when I was much younger, my parents would gift me with books that seemed really mature for me. Books like *Think and Grow Rich* and *How to Win Friends and Influence People* were given to me to read. In order to help me get through them, they would also buy them on audio so I could listen to the books as I fell asleep. After listening to such awesome words of wisdom, I got pumped and ready to take on the world with my business. It helped me to develop success principles and disciplines I could use my whole life. So that's what I went back to doing. While in college, I got books on audio that I could listen to. This was like the best invention ever created because I was able to get the knowledge I needed at a much faster and easier rate.

Why is Reading so Important, Ari?

The more successful you become, the more you will have to read. Why? Because reading holds the key to your next level in business, and in your life. There are secrets that are laid out in books that could answer the very question you need to make your next business deal, launch your online course or get your product in that store. My mom, Dr. Stacia Pierce, always says that successful people leave clues. I believe this all to be true. Successful others want people to do well in life, so they put hints in books and audiotapes about how they have made it big. They aren't going to just give out those precious gems for free, so it means that you have to make an investment to get the secrets to true success.

Activity/Assignment: Book List

That's why for the next 30 days, I want you to read or listen to a new book per week. I've created a worksheet below that will help you to look for success clues in each book you read.

Worksheet: Write out the books you are going to read. Then write out a success clue(s) you found while reading or listening to your new books. Once you are finished, go over them to see how these clues can help you move forward your business.

Name of book I'm reading: Success secret that will help me in business:

1. _____   _____

2. _____   _____

3. _____   _____

4. _____   _____

5. _____   _____

6. _____   _____

7. _____   _____

8. _____   _____

9. _____   _____

10. _____   _____

CHAPTER 8

FINDING LOVE AS AN
ENTREPRENEUR

As a kid who wasn't allowed to seriously date until about the age of 18 years old, I found myself imagining and daydreaming about my perfect mate just about every single day. I come from a family that values marriage and family, so this was a big deal to me. I wanted to find a prince charming who was strong, handsome and respectful to me and my parents. When I closed my eyes, I would see a tall, strong and handsome man with lots of personality. I had no problem with being in a mixed-race relationship, so my dream guy was anyone who would love me. He would one day sweep me off my feet. We would fall madly in love and get married in no time. We would spend a few years together—about five—just to enjoy each other and travel the world. We would then have our first child around the age of 26 and then have another before the age of 30. It was the perfect love story and I was Cinderella waiting for Mr. Prince Charming to find me.

Well, that didn't happen, and here's the real story: When I started my first year at Michigan State University, I was an entrepreneur and very focused. The dream of a fairytale love story at age 20 was pushed back a bit, and I didn't have time to worry about guys because I was busy. Plus, I hadn't been used to a serious relationship so it didn't bother me.

After some time went on and I got a handle on school and running a full-time business, I was ready to meet my lover. I opened up and began to look for love. I grew up pretty traditional, so I held the idea of a man approaching me and asking me out on a date. Whether that's old-fashioned or not, I didn't care; it was what I believed.

Over time, I began to hang around a lot of athletes. I wasn't the girl who slept with them at all; I was the girl who was their friend. Now, if you went to a college with a good football or basketball team, then you know that these were the popular guys that ruled campus. I would like to think that my popularity went up from being best friends with them. Anyway, over time, I grew an attraction toward one of them. We began to talk and hang out just about every day. We would go grocery shopping, go to the movies and hang out. This wasn't just a regular friendship—we talked about being together and dating requirements that each of us expected. Over time, people knew that we were "dating," but it was still casual.

I remember it like yesterday: We went to the movies, had a great time and chatted about our future. He told me goodnight and everything was fine. Well, a few days later, I walk into the cafeteria where we always ate and saw him eating and having an intimate conversation with another girl. This took me by surprise. I went over to his table unashamedly to check it out. He quickly said, "What's up FRIEND, how are you? This is my girlfriend from New Jersey," and introduced us.

I had a choice to be messy and say, "Oh, this is your girlfriend? That's funny because last night we were just on a date." That's exactly what went through my mind, but I decided to be mature and say nothing. I later confronted him about the situation and totally cut it off. What I didn't know at that moment was that I would have a few more experiences just like this in my life before finding someone who had the right motives and really cared for me.

I later dated a guy whom I had met at an event. He was awesome, full of life and loved coming to visit my family. Things were going great for a long time. I was now one to take my time in relationships to avoid getting hurt like in the past. As he began to learn more about what I had to offer, I found him pulling away toward the end. After one visit in particular, he left to go back home, said farewell and I didn't hear from him anymore. *What? How could this be? Nothing was wrong*, I thought.

I wasn't an easy girl. I didn't sleep around. As a matter of fact, I'm saving myself for my husband. And I wasn't a messy girl. Over time, the guys I dated said that I was kind, loving and their ideal "girl". So what was the problem? I began to doubt myself and wonder if I wasn't cool enough or just too traditional. Well, I would soon find out the answer.

I began to look over my life and ask why? Why were these guys super attracted to me but once they got to know me, fell back? Well, I finally got the answer: Someone revealed to me that it was nothing I was doing wrong, but it was intimidation that made them dash away. *Intimidation of what?* I thought. The intimidation that comes with dating a girl who is already on top of her career, doing business, flying to speak at conferences on the weekend and gaining national exposure for her brand.

I was astonished when I heard these things. These guys were college students or everyday guys who were attracted to my success, but when they had to witness it up close, they felt as if they couldn't offer me much. They would have rather been with a girl they could easily impress or keep up with instead. This made me rethink relationships and marriage for girls out there who are girl bosses and making major moves. What were we to do? The next thing was to find a guy who was also doing big things and was a successful entrepreneur, but then they seemed to want girls who were there to totally help them with their business endeavors. What about when you both have big dreams?

The Solution

You may be a girl boss who is looking for your perfect soul mate. That was definitely on my mind and has been since I've been a little girl. Over time, I realized that it was a bit harder for those of us who are achieving a lot at a young age. With men's egos, I wondered if I had to give up being an entrepreneur and achieving my goals in order to find a mate who would really love and support my career. You may be wondering the same thing. Maybe you have had a hard time finding a guy (or a girl, for the guys) who will support you and be OK with your success-driven lifestyle, because work is life!

A relationship with a 9-to-5 person may not work if you are an entrepreneur. Just so we are clear, a 9-to-5 person is someone who not only works a standard job, but it's someone who believes that work ends right at 5 pm. Once the time hits, all work is put to the side and real life begins with relaxation, laughs and dinner. Though none of this is bad, it can cause tension in your relationship. When work and life are separated, it can be difficult to understand an entrepreneur's lifestyle.

So the BIG question is: Is it possible to do both your career *and* find a love that's strong? Of course! You just have to believe that it's possible, AND you have to go for a different type of person. What do I mean by this? Well, if you are a girl who keeps going for the same type of guys and getting the same results, then you are going to have to change something—whether it's attracting a guy with different kind of personality, outlook on life, or finding a more mature man. Whatever the situation, you have to do something different in order to get different results out of your relationship.

That's exactly what I did. Before, I was going for all the "cool cats," as my dad would call them: guys who wanted to be smooth and wanted all the attention. Once I found out that this type of guy wouldn't mesh well with my lifestyle, I had to look for something different. I know right now this may sound like it sucks. You like what you like, right? But sometimes what we want right now isn't the best option for our future and progress. Trust me, once you change your standards and requirements, you will begin to attract the perfect match for you. Once you see how this NEW type of guy (or girl) treats, loves and supports you, you'll wonder why you didn't find this person sooner.

Like I mentioned, as an entrepreneur, work is life. It's a part of who you are and what you do. You have to get with someone who understands the entrepreneur's way of life; otherwise, they could become frustrated and find themselves battling for your time and the attention that you will sometimes have to give to your career. It can result in them even blaming your work for getting in the way. What's wrong here is that your love for a person can be so strong that their misunderstanding of your lifestyle can cause you to get off focus from your life's calling, and you'll find yourself scaling back for them. I'm not saying having time to focus on your relationship is bad, but you have to be sure you are in a place of peace when it comes to your love life and work. Both can happen successfully when you require the right type of person!

What Are the New Requirements?

Now that you have read my words on finding a new type of mate who will support your endeavors as an entrepreneur, there is no way I wasn't going to leave you with insight on what these new requirements should be. In this section I have compiled a list of things to look for as a boss lady (or boss man) who wants to find love.

1. **Take your time.** As a person building your empire, you want to take your time when getting into relationships. See what the person is all about and their motives for dating you. Never feel like you have to rush into a relationship to keep a person. If they really like you and want to be with you, they will wait for you!

2. **Look for signs.** When dating, look for signs that

could be a hindrance or contribute to your success. If you find that your significant other doesn't celebrate or cheer when you have successes, that's a sign of jealousy. A person who loves and is happy for you will celebrate you big and push you to do more. Will they defend you when people or obstacles come your way, or will they leave you stranded? A person who's for you will stick with you when the going gets tough (if you aren't doing anything illegal, of course). On the other hand, they should be there to correct you when you are wrong and help you get on course. It's called an accountability partner—someone you can be accountable to in your career and in personal life. For example, my father keeps my mother accountable by telling her to get her rest. Though my mom can burn the midnight oil, it doesn't always yield the best return if she gets fatigued. So my father steps in to keep her on track so she can be the best entrepreneur she can be!

3. **Get someone who complements you.** Find someone who is a complement to your success. This doesn't mean that you don't help them with their career or endeavors, but it does mean that you flow in harmony together. A couple that can help build each other up is truly unstoppable. In a relationship, you both will have your own purpose, hobbies and likes, but they should complement each other and bring lots of value to the partnership.

4. **Get a "Get It" partner.** A Get It partner is someone who understands the life of an entrepreneur. Even if he or she isn't one, they understand the role and time it takes

to build an empire. As a boss, there will be late nights in the office, time away from family and potentially lots of travel depending on the field of business. It's a must that your significant other understands this, or it could be a very big problem in the future. The life of an entrepreneur is very different from a person who works a 9 am to 5 pm job, but the rewards are very big as well. I would suggest testing out late nights in the office or busy days to see how they react. Another thing you can do is just tell your significant other about the lifestyle you lead. Let them know about the late nights in the office, business trips and the time it takes to be an entrepreneur. My father always told me that entrepreneurship equals inconvenience. That means that you may get an order that has to be filled at 3 am or you may get an invitation to go speak in the Bahamas last minute. Either way, it can be an inconvenience to previous plans. The number one thing that your partner should master is flexibility and patience. Both will help the relationship a lot!

5. **Morals are important.** This is the biggest requirement that I would suggest you stick to. Never ever compromise your beliefs or standards for someone unless they are for your good. I say that because sometimes we hold on to beliefs that are hindering us instead of helping us. On the other hand, find a companion who is willing to be honest, trustworthy and has integrity. Being in business means dealing with money, clients and even the law. Having someone whom you can truly trust is important to the success in your relationship and your brand.

Activity/Assignment: **The List**

Create a list of desires and deal-breakers for your relationship. Make two columns—one should be the desires side; the other should be deal-breakers. Deal-breakers are things you can never see yourself living with. For example, you may want someone tall, but your deal-breaker could be someone who hates to travel. The great thing about writing what you don't like is that you are able to see what you really want out of a relationship and partner. Below you will see an example of my list and how I discovered what I really wanted in a guy!

Notes

Desires	Deal-breakers
- A Giver.	- Someone who's Selfish.
- Affectionate.	- Someone who Complains.
- Christian	- A bitter person.
- Has goals/dreams.	- Doesn't like my Entrepreneurial
- Loves to travel	lifestyle.

CHAPTER 9

TAKE ME TO CHURCH

Life as a pastor's kid was not the easiest. Growing up in a family that was fully involved in ministry was great, but the judgment that came with it was the tough part. I've been a church girl ever since I can remember. Every Sunday, we would get dressed up in our best to attend church. The Word was exactly what got me through tough times in my life, school and in business.

As a pastor's kid, AKA a "PK," it was a life in a glass house. Everyone was watching what I was doing. On one hand, it was as if I was an example to those who came to church, if I did what they thought was right. On the other hand, I was a troubled and misled kid if I did something that didn't match their criteria for being a Christian.

As I began to grow older, I discovered that I couldn't live my life to please others, but I had to live my life to please God, my family and myself. Once I broke free from the bondage of trying to be perfect, I was able to really begin manifesting my dreams and goals.

When I began to do business and business coaching, it shocked the church world. They hadn't seen too many PKs go into full-time business, and it surprised them. Criticism came my way for a few years and I heard things like, "You aren't Christian enough," or, "You should be preaching instead of business." I had two choices: listen to them and fall to their opinion, or do what God told me to in this world by impacting lives through entrepreneurship.

I chose to continue my calling of inspiring young people around the world to live their dreams now and not later. Over time, I found that the same people criticizing me for going a different route started to venture into business and entrepreneurship. It was as if I was the front-runner who took the hit, but over time made it OK for other PKs to branch out from the norm.

I'm not saying that it's wrong to do ministry. I'm actually doing ministry, just in a different way. I believe that your ministry is your calling—whether it be a doctor, lawyer, manager, business coach, entrepreneur or pastor, you can live your life in a way that inspires others to be their best.

Faith

Faith has helped me in my toughest times. I'm not talking about your profession of faith; I'm talking about the type of faith that gives you hope when you can't see how the end will play out—the type of faith that helps you keep pushing, knowing that something good is going to happen for you and turn into your favor.

I know this to be very true in my personal life. One day, I received a call from a very important TV network. They are actually one of the top stations in the world, and they were at the beginning stages of launching one of their first reality TV shows. They had heard a lot about my brand, Superstar Nail Lacquer, from other Hollywood insiders and knew that we would be fit for the job.

Weeks went by and we had come to an agreement to have Superstar Nail Lacquer create a custom line for the TV show that was coming out. Just like they have special makeup collaborations for movies, that's exactly what it was going to be like for us, except this time it was on TV instead of a movie. Things were going great as we began to actually roll out the inventory that would be sold all around the world. We came up with custom colors and names to match the characters on the show and this was going to be the biggest deal our company had done at the time.

It was going perfectly until a few days later, we got a call that changed everything. We picked up the phone, eager and excited to finalize the project, when suddenly, the network said, "We are sorry to do this to you at the last minute, but we aren't going to do the deal with you." I immediately cleared my ears to be sure I heard right. Yes, they reneged at the last second because they "didn't think we were fit." Umm, well ... you should have told us that before we had more than 10,000 bottles of polish made with custom names specifically for the show.

At this moment, I had no real answers. I needed a lot of *faith* to sell these extra thousands of bottles of polish that I had, on top of our regular collection. We had spent so much money in preparation for the deal, and we had to change the entire concept of the collection, being that we couldn't use the show as a selling point anymore or we would get sued. I prayed, meditated and wrote in my journal by asking God questions on what I should do and how I should go about selling this extra inventory. As I continued to write, the answers came to me daily on strategic marketing plans that helped us to make and recover well over the amount we spent on this bad deal.

Though I was disappointed in the beginning, it was my faith that gave me an anchor to not give up even though things didn't go my way. I mean, a lot happened here: Not only did the deal not go through and we had so much inventory to sell, but the company actually stated that they didn't want to finish the deal because they didn't think I was fit to handle it. That could have easily affected my self-esteem as a 20-something-year-old trying to run her business and get a handle on life. I chose not to give up and to fight the good fight. Now, some of those same people who doubted me are calling upon me for business advice. Boy, how the tables turn when you stay on track!

Finding The Solution

I believe that all things can work for your good when you keep the right attitude and you remain grateful. When the deal with the network failed, I didn't stop doing business for good because there was a moment that seemed like failure. I decided to just do something different. Like I mentioned, I began to write and journalize and the opportunity came for me to get my products into boutiques and stores. Our products can be found in Brazil and I even got the opportunity to provide my Alma Mater, Michigan State University, with Go Green nail lacquer that does phenomenally well. I went from just going to MSU, to doing business with MSU. So no, I didn't get the original deal, but now I get to meet so many fabulous entrepreneurs and business owners who retail my products. This is why it's so important to let go of the fear of failure, and embrace new opportunities that can launch you into higher levels of success than you ever thought was possible.

Activity/Assignment: Overcome Your Fears With Faith

This chapter was all about taking a leap of faith to go after your goals. I want you to create a list of things that have been hindering you from either starting your business or things that have stopped you from taking your business to the next level. Once you have your list, I want you to write and take action on those fears by going after them. For example, if you are afraid to start your business because you don't have enough money, I want you get past that fear by starting a savings account to acquire the money necessary for your business. If you believe that not having enough knowledge of business is holding you back, then get past the fear by hiring a business coach. Faith without works is dead. So in order to be in good faith, we have to take action on our fears to get past them and to become victorious in our lives.

Hinderance List

Fear: Actions Steps to Overcome Fear:

1. _____   _____

2. _____   _____

3. _____   _____

4. _____   _____

5. _____   _____

6. _____   _____

7. _____   _____

8. _____   _____

9. _____   _____

10. _____   _____

Notes: _____

_____

_____

_____

_____

_____

CHAPTER 10

TIME AWAY FROM THE USA

While in college, I had the opportunity to travel abroad. I was heading into my junior year at Michigan State University and needed some extra credits to stay on track for my goal of graduating in exactly four years. Though that's not required, I wanted to be done with college so I could use all of my energy and focus on my business and speaking.

I went to talk to one of my favorite advisors about what I should do to get more credits for the semester. As we sat and talked for a while, she said, "You know what, I have an idea. You should really think about studying abroad in Japan for the summer. It'll give you more than enough credits to keep you on track for graduating in just four years, and you'll get a life-changing experience." After we talked, I took the booklet that had the information and considered doing exactly what she had said. I must admit that I was a bit nervous, being that I hadn't been out the country without at least a friend or relative. This time around, it would be just me with students I didn't really know. But after more convincing from one of my mom's assistants, I signed up for the Japan study abroad program and I was accepted.

Boy, was I excited to head to Asia for the first time. While counting the days until I left for this awesome trip, I had the opportunity to go to London and Paris for spring break with some friends. I had put on my vision board that year that it would be the year of travel, and it definitely was.

While I was sitting in the hotel room in London, I get news of a great tsunami that hit Japan and unfortunately, my plans to Japan were canceled. In that moment, I was very disappointed, but at the same time very thankful that the disaster didn't happen while I, or any of the other students coming along, were in Japan. In the email, they presented the opportunity to go to Europe for the summer and that's exactly what I chose. A few months later, I found myself on the plane and off to Paris, Rome, Florence, and Cinque Terra. When I tell you this was the best decision I made at that time, it really was.

Stepping foot in Paris without my parents and without anyone I really knew was scary. Being thousands of miles away from family and friends was something to get used to, but it challenged me to really be independent and explore the world for myself. After a few days of being homesick, the feeling left and I made a decision to not only sightsee in these amazing countries, but to really take something home with me that would expand my mind.

Everything was going smoothly while abroad and I was having many amazing experiences. One thing that I began to notice, however, was that we had to make continuous stops by the U.S. Embassy. So many students in my group were losing their passports or travel documents because they had their things disorganized—and of course were freaking out because they wanted to get back home safely. Who wouldn't be worried about their one document that could get them back home to their family? It sparked an idea in me that later turned into one of my most profitable businesses.

Once I returned home and was back at Michigan State University, I studied hard and made sure to get good grades for the remaining semesters, using my focus to build up Superstar Nail Lacquer and my speaking career. The memories from studying abroad were so amazing that I decided to do another short program to London, England. With that experience, I found myself loving travel and wishing that more girls like me could see and explore the world and its amazing cultures, food and people. It sparked an idea in me that would come to fruition years later.

Fast-forward after graduation and I was sitting in my office, looking through inventory that we had in stock. I saw that there were passport covers from my line that we had for a special season but after that, I hadn't paid much attention to them. It was something that I used for my own travels, but I never really thought that my current audience would demand them. In spite of that, I put them online for sale and the passports sold out in minutes. It was an unbelievable response and I knew that I had something valuable.

Soon after that, I decided to redesign the passport covers with special inserts so that those who were traveling wouldn't lose their passport, license or travel documents. The inspiration came from my travels abroad and seeing so many people misplace their important things. I knew that if the passport cover was bright, pretty and could fit everything a traveler needs, then it would be a hot item. That's exactly what happened: They became amazingly popular and are now one of our most profitable businesses.

This is why I believe that exposure creates desire, and desire leads to profits. When you take the time to get outside of your neighborhood, usual environment and everyday group of people, you open yourself up to be inspired in a way like never before. If I had never taken that trip abroad, I would not have considered making a passport cover that would keep your travel documents safe and in one place. I would have never thought to make them bright and fabulous for the traveling fashionista. Something was sparked in me years before creating it, and now it's one of my passions. You see, it's more than just a cute passport cover, it's a brand that encourages girls to step outside of their comfort zone to see the world around them. I've used my passion for travel to inspire others around the world to see their potential and help inspire another.

Activity/Assignment: Travel Plans

Now I want you to think outside the box! As mentioned above, traveling expands your mind and helps you to be more creative. Take a moment to think of some places you can visit that will expose you to greatness and cause you to dream bigger.

For example, visiting a museum, the White House, or the Eiffel Tower are all places that can help inspire your future plans or next business venture. Use the following page to list places that you plan to visit for inspiration!

Top 10 Places I Would Love to Travel To

1. _____

2. _____

3. _____

4. _____

5. _____

6. _____

7. _____

8. _____

9. _____

10. _____

Notes: _____

_____

_____

_____

_____

_____

CONCLUSION: YOU DID IT!

S o you've come to the end of the book and finished all your assignments or activities. Congratulations! It's now your time to launch over into the deep and go after your dreams of being that successful entrepreneur.

Whether you are just starting out, or you've been in business for years, I want to encourage you to keep striving for your dreams until they become your reality. Just like I had bullies and people who tried to discourage me from living my best life, there may be people just like that on your path who don't understand your hustle and drive. That's okay, but I would advise you to get away from them. Don't be rude, but nicely remove yourself from their influence of doubt and complacency. It's a must that you begin to surround yourself with others who have the same mindset and goals as you. I call them "get it" friends: People who get your life, your dedication and determination.

I want you to know that if no one else does, I believe in you 100%. I believe that you were created for something big. You are not mistake, but you have purpose and destiny on the inside of you. What's so funny is that most of your purpose isn't for you. It's to help inspire someone else to live their dreams now and not later. Instead of thinking about how hard it is to stay focused on your goals, think about how hard it'll be for someone else if you don't fulfill those goals. Someone is waiting for you to show him or her the way. That's exactly why I felt it was time to write this book. I was doing business for me, which isn't a bad thing, but one day I woke up with a vision to do business to help inspire. I know that's exactly what you want for others as well.

So stop with the excuses. Get off your butt and start making some things happen. Start that t-shirt business. Build that tech company. Create the next big app. Whatever it is you choose, do it with your whole heart and keep going until you see the victory. Forget all the partying every weekend. Use that time to build your business and brand now, so you can party all you want later...and with lots of money. Get ready, Get set, GO!

Other Products
by Ariana Pierce

I Deserve It All – Travelpreneur Kit

For the woman who's heart is in travel! The I deserve it all kit comes with the travel journal, travelpreneur's affirmation cards and passport cover (which comes in an array of beautiful candy colors) so that you are always prepared to travel in style. **The Travel Journal,** included in this kit was inspired from my own travel dreams and love for culture. It's a journal that helps you visualize where you want to go and remember the destinations you have already explored.

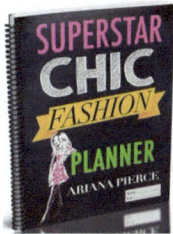

Superstar Chic Fashion Planner

In just minutes per day, Ariana will show you how to create a successful, organized fashion blog with the power of a planner! When used correctly, a fashion calendar can instantly help you stay organized, plan your wardrobe and remain consistent and productive which ultimately leads to profits. This planner will help you stay consistent and prompts you with intriguing questions to keep your daily image and blogging on track.

Travelpreneur Affirmation Cards

Have you ever dreamed of traveling the world? The Travelpreneur Affirmation Cards are designed to help you manifest your dream vacation, destination and adventures. Each card comes with an area to paste pictures of your dream destination as well as an affirmation created by Ariana Pierce, that she has used over the years to manifest many dream trips of her own. One being going to Europe multiple times in a year. Manifest your dream trip and order your affirmation cards today!

TO ORDER, VISIT:
Arianapierce.com
SuperstarNailLacquer.com
Styleshoppe.com
OR CALL: 1-888-484-7543

www.ingramcontent.com/pod-product-compliance
Lightning Source LLC
Chambersburg PA
CBHW041713200326
41519CB00001B/144